Original title:
The Pear's Whisper

Copyright © 2025 Creative Arts Management OÜ
All rights reserved.

Author: Thomas Sinclair
ISBN HARDBACK: 978-1-80586-371-7
ISBN PAPERBACK: 978-1-80586-843-9

Unveiling Nature's Gifts

In the garden, fruits collide,
Chasing dreams with skins so wide.
Bananas slip, giggling on the floor,
While berries blush, longing for more.

Apples chat with a playful breeze,
Cracking jokes among the trees.
Lemons laugh at every twist,
Zesty puns that can't be missed.

Crisp cucumbers in a conga line,
Dancing to a rhythm, all divine.
Radishes roll, trying to outpace,
Their leafy friends in a silly race.

In this world where veggies glow,
And fruits wear hats, just for show.
Nature giggles, a funny rift,
Come, enjoy her playful gift!

Riddles of the Skin

What's round, yet wears a coat?
And giggles when you poke its throat?
A riddle ripe and full of cheer,
It tickles taste buds, oh so near.

With a twist, it gleams like gold,
Whispers stories yet untold.
A puzzle fresh from orchard's hand,
Come unravel this fruit so grand!

The Allure of Juicy Dreams

In visions bright, they bounce and sway,
Sweet temptations that beg you to stay.
A splash of juice will spark the fun,
It dances in delight, oh what a pun!

Dreams take flight in fruity schemes,
Each bite delivers silly screams.
A zesty giggle, a burst of cheer,
One juicy dream, let's make it clear!

Beneath the Green Veil

Underneath a leafy tangle,
Lies a secret that makes us dangle.
With a wink, it bursts so bright,
Filling moments with pure delight.

What hides beneath the emerald shade?
A treasure trove where fun is made.
It shakes and giggles through the trees,
A playful fruit that aims to please!

Serene Conversations of Branches

Branches chatter, twist, and twirl,
Silly secrets they unfurl.
A fruit swings in, grinning wide,
It joins the chat, can't slip aside.

"I'm juicy!," it declares with glee,
"Come slice me up, let's have some tea!"
With laughter ripe and voices loud,
Nature's quirky, juicy crowd!

Shimmering Underneath the Branches

Buzzing bees take their chance,
While squirrels plot in a dance.
A fruit with giggles, oh my!
It hides secrets both sweet and spry.

Chirping birds pass a nudge,
"What's the fruit's next little grudge?"
Laughter spills with each bright shade,
As secrets in the sun cascade.

Secrets Beneath the Ripe Canopy.

Green globes hang, what a sight,
Hiding tales both merry and light.
A fruit declaring its zest,
While ants march in a grand fest.

"It's not just juicy," one crow caws,
"Fruit diplomacy has its laws!"
Beneath the leaves, whispers reign,
With giggles that dance in the grain.

Fruits of Secrets

Beneath the shade where laughter grows,
Fruits debate while the wind blows.
A berry winks with a cheeky grin,
While apples scheme, "Let's pull a win!"

Ripe plums giggle, what a tease,
Making wishes on the breeze.
"Who'd like to play a little prank?"
As sunlight spills into the bank.

Echoes in the Orchard

The orchard hums with cheer and jest,
Fruits in a riddle, quite the quest.
"Guess my flavor!" a peach declares,
While cherries giggle up in pairs.

Whispers dart like fireflies round,
In this lively, fruity playground.
With every chuckle, ripeness is clear,
As laughter sprouts, year after year.

Beneath the Branches' Shade

In the garden where the fruit spies,
Giggling leaves with clever eyes.
Chasing shadows, laughs cascade,
Under branches, secrets laid.

Silly squirrels in a race,
Stash their nuts without a trace.
The breeze joins in, it starts to sway,
Whispering jokes that drift away.

The Essence of Quiet Harvest

Beneath the boughs, a dance of cheek,
Fruits in whispers, words unique.
With every pluck, a giggle felt,
They chuckle soft as sunlight melts.

Crickets chirp, a comic show,
As sunlight begins to glow.
Whimsical tunes of nature's band,
Tickling toes in the soft land.

Body and Soul of the Orchard

In the orchard, truce is sweet,
As fruits gather for a treat.
Grapes gossip, apples roll,
Orange peels take on a stroll.

Pears play tag, oh what a sight,
Ripe with laughter, pure delight.
Underneath the friendly sky,
All the fruits conspire and sigh.

The Conclusion of Summer's Symphony

As the summer bids goodbye,
With gusto, fruits begin to fly.
A melody of rustling leaves,
Compose the humor that believes.

With every drop, a story told,
Of sunshine moments, bright and bold.
In berry blush and melon grin,
They waltz and giggle, the harvest wins.

Hidden Songs of the Grove

In the grove, where shadows play,
Fruits plot mischief every day.
Apples giggle, oranges cheer,
While bananas make jokes sincere.

Grapes roll laughter down the lane,
Cherries dance, avoiding rain.
They whisper tales of juicy pranks,
Amidst their sweet, round, fruity ranks.

Squirrels pause to join the fun,
As acorns drop, one by one.
The breeze carries quirky tunes,
Echoing beneath the moons.

So if you stroll through leaf and vine,
Listen closely, you might find,
Songs of fruit, both bright and bold,
In the grove, where tales are told.

Gentle Rumors of the Wind

Whispers float on breezy flights,
Carrying gags from leafy heights.
Berries gossip, teasing shy,
While melons wink as they pass by.

The wind sings tales of forts and dreams,
With fizzy laughs and silly themes.
Every breeze a chuckle shared,
With cheeky fruit unprepared.

Mangoes snicker, pears roll by,
With playful winks that catch the eye.
Nature's jesters in the sun,
Spreading joy as they all run.

So if you feel a gentle sway,
Join in laughter, don't delay.
For in the whispers of the trees,
You'll find humor in the breeze.

Laughter of the Sun-Kissed Leaves

Sun-kissed leaves begin to sway,
Tickling branches in the play.
Limes and lemons giggle sweet,
While peaches dance on tiny feet.

With every rustle, secrets bloom,
Bright laughter fills the sunny room.
Pineapple jokes, oh so divine,
Crack them open with some wine.

The rhythm of the roots below,
Echoes laughter that we know.
Fruits unite in joyful song,
Together where they all belong.

So twirl among the vibrant greens,
Join the fun, slip into scenes.
In this world where joy is rife,
You'll find the funny side of life.

Conversations Among the Fruit Baskets

In baskets piled, a chatter grows,
As every fruit in friendship knows.
Raspberries tease the plump, round pears,
While avocados share silly glares.

The oranges roll with laughter loud,
Applauding berries, proudly bowed.
Kiwi jokes with zest and flair,
Bouncing off the woven air.

Each fruit's tale a comical twist,
With mischief that can't be dismissed.
Pineapples burst with giggles bright,
As laughter echoes through the night.

So next time you reach for a snack,
Remember laughter's cheerful track.
For in the fruit basket's delight,
Humor ripens, oh so right.

Whispers From the Ground

In a garden where veggies conspire,
Carrots gossip, and greens never tire.
Tomatoes blush, hidden under leaves,
As radishes chuckle, plotting their thieves.

A cucumber winks, snug in the soil,
While garlic dances, fragrant and loyal.
Potatoes giggle, beneath their gray shroud,
As laughter erupts from the whispering crowd.

Chronicles of the Orchard's Heart

Branches sway with tales yet untold,
Where apples joke, and secrets unfold.
Cherries chuckle in their ruby-red gowns,
While oranges boast of their sunny crowns.

Pears hide their laughter, round and so sweet,
While lemons squabble, all sour with heat.
In this orchard, mirth grows on every vine,
As nature's comedy unfolds, oh so fine.

The Enchantment of Juicy Fruits

A watermelon giggles, bursting with cheer,
While peaches shimmy, bringing good beer.
Berries tease, in their colorful packs,
Their juicy jokes leave us all in cracks.

Bananas slip into laughter's embrace,
As grapes roll around, keeping up their pace.
Nature's stand-up, in shades so bright,
A fruity fiesta, pure delight!

The Graces of a Bountiful Day

With sunshine showering the garden's array,
Every vegetable jigs in a playful display.
Lettuce laughs, sprouting with flair,
While radishes blush, hiding under hair.

Mangoes gossip beneath swaying trees,
Kiwis exchange their hilarious tease.
It's a harvest of joy, filled with delight,
In this quirky world, everything feels right.

Hushed Conversations of the Trees

In the garden, secrets flow,
Leaves giggle, whispers grow.
Branches sway in playful jest,
Tickled by the breezy quest.

Squirrels pause, with ears perked high,
Eavesdropping on tales that fly.
Rabbits hop with knowing grins,
Hiding snickers in their dens.

Breezes dance through leafy crowns,
Telling jokes in leafy towns.
The wise old oak, with bark so strong,
Shares puns that make the forest long.

Under stars, they share a laugh,
'Why did the tree take a bath?'
Nobody knows, but who could care,
When laughter echoes through the air?

The Covert Joys of Gathering

Gather 'round, the fruit brigade,
In hushed tones, plans are laid.
A picnic spread, with crumbs galore,
Who knew fruit could crave some more?

Grapes wear hats, so dapper and fine,
Bantering softly, sipping sunshine.
A rogue pineapple slips on a peel,
Causing the lemons to squeal and feel.

The giggles roll through stems and vines,
With every joke, the sun brightly shines.
As apples chuckle in shades of red,
They roll around, the loudest spread.

But shh! Keep it down, don't let it spill,
Just a fruit party on yonder hill.
When the farmer comes, we all shall hide,
In laughter and kinship, we joyfully bide.

Sweet Confessions of the Branches

Branches shiver, sharing dreams,
Gossip floats like honeyed creams.
One boasts of a butterfly's kiss,
"Just don't let the bees suspect this!"

A wise old limb spills tales of old,
Of summer fires and stories bold.
"Once I held a squirrel's first leap,
Secret laughs we still keep."

Each twig has secret rendezvous,
With raccoons, owls, and morning dews.
As shadows dance beneath the light,
They confess their mischief, pure delight.

"Who dropped that acorn?" one calls loud,
As laughter rings through bough and crowd.
In whispered tones and softest shade,
The secrets of the woods are laid.

Under the Weight of Bounty

Under the load, vines twist and sway,
Fruits tumble down to play their way.
Orchard's laughter fills the air,
As apples roll without a care.

"Watch out for the melon!" one fruit yells,
As berries giggle, casting spells.
Plums stick out, proud on their perch,
While oranges plot a juicy search.

Jugs run wild by the breezy lane,
Fruits in unison, a merry train.
Harvest time, a rollicking race,
In the festival of fruit-filled grace.

With barrels rolling, laughter soars,
Who knew bounty could knock on doors?
Under this load, we all unite,
In a funny saga, oh what a sight!

In the Quiet Sunlight

In sunlight's hug, the fruit does grin,
A cheeky smile, where mischief begins.
Laughter floats on branches high,
A fruit's joke under the blue sky.

Squirrels gawk, eyes open wide,
As sunlight dances, they cannot hide.
A plump pear does a jig, quite spry,
While bees hum along, oh my!

Beneath the leaves, the whispers start,
Jokes exchanged, a fruity art.
With every giggle, the orchard sways,
In sunlight sweet, we laugh away.

Secrets Among the Foliage

In leafy confines, secrets unfold,
Stories of fruit so vividly told.
A grape winks at a pear nearby,
While apples snicker, oh my, oh my!

Beneath the twigs, giggles sprout,
What's this riddle? Let's figure it out!
A fruit's dare to take a leap,
With humorous ploys that never sleep.

The rustling leaves share a prank,
A mischievous pie who's sobered by rank.
With each rustle, a chuckle appears,
Among the foliage, joy never veers.

The Sigh of Pollinated Dreams

In buzzing dreams, the flowers sway,
They chuckle, "Guess who's here to play?"
With pollen dusted, they bloom with glee,
A matchmaker's dance of nectar and bee.

Bees wiggle and tickle in floral beds,
"Get in line!" the petals said.
With a laugh, they spin and twirl,
As wishes of fruit take flight and whirl.

Jokes unpeeled, like skins of good fun,
Pollinated schemes, oh what a run!
Nature's giggles, the sweetest scheme,
Among the blossoms, laughter's theme.

Enigmas of Orchard Paths

On crooked paths where mischief roams,
Fruitful riddles find their homes.
A pear hides behind a leafy wall,
"Can you catch me?" it dares to call.

In shadows deep, the jokes take flight,
As mushrooms giggle in the pale moonlight.
"Oh, what's green and juicy and sly?"
An orchard's riddle, oh my, oh my!

With every step, a chuckle thrives,
As vines weave tales and laughter arrives.
In twists and turns, the fun unwinds,
Amongst the trees, what joy one finds!

Whispers in the Garden's Heart

In the garden, secrets dance,
While the bees play a clumsy romance.
The daisies giggle, the tulips grin,
As mischievous fairies tuck in their kin.

The carrots gossip, the onions whisper,
Telling tales of the sneaky drifter.
A squirrel with acorns, a cheeky stunt,
Hiding his treasures, a rascally hunt.

Beneath the leaves, the rabbits jest,
Hosting a feast, they're quite the guests.
With lettuce crowns, they prance around,
Dance like nobody's watching, not a sound.

So in this garden, where laughter blooms,
Even the soil hums with fun tunes.
Let the veggies giggle and the flowers sing,
In this cheerful realm, joy is the king.

Stories Woven in Fragrance

Lavender scents float through the air,
While rosemary plots a charming affair.
The thyme is up to some cheeky prank,
As lilacs twirl at the garden's bank.

Peppermint chuckles, bold and bright,
Tickling noses with fragrant delight.
A whiff of danger from the basil bold,
Stealing the show, it's a sight to behold.

The petals gossip with fragrant flair,
Telling of bees and their sweet affair.
Each bloom's a tale, a quirky spin,
In the world of scents, let the stories begin.

As dusk approaches, scents intertwine,
Making mischief with every vine.
In this fragrant chaos, laughter we find,
With each whiff, a little joy combined.

Hush of Autumn's Bounty

In autumn's hush, pumpkins grin wide,
As acorns roll down the slide.
The leaves, like giggly kids, take flight,
In twirling dances, a comical sight.

The apple tree sighs with a fruity laugh,
As the cider spills, pouring a gaffe.
The bees buzz low, wearing tiny hats,
Joining the fun with the charm of chitchats.

Squirrels are plotting, a nutty scheme,
Gathering treasures, living the dream.
While in the background, a crow's loud caw,
Turns to laughter with a silly guffaw.

So gather 'round for the autumn cheer,
With harvest smiles, let's raise a beer.
In nature's bounty, where joy takes its stand,
Every whimsy and chuckle, perfectly planned.

Suspended Notes in Green

A breeze of giggles flutters by,
As leaves chatter, exchanging a sigh.
In treetops, where the sunshine beams,
The world spins 'round in whimsical dreams.

Each leaf a note in nature's song,
Harmonizing where they belong.
A caterpillar jokes on a leafy path,
Making the flowers burst into laugh.

The brook babbles with tales so wry,
As fish splash up, flinging dry.
Under the sun's golden gleam,
Nature conspires to make us beam.

So find your joy in this lush spread,
Where laughter dances, and worries shed.
With every rustle, a catchy tune,
In this green sanctuary, silliness blooms.

Sweet Secrets of the Harvest

In the orchard, gossip flows,
Beneath the branches, laughter grows.
Fruit debates on whose juice is best,
Apples boast, but pears don't rest.

Wind tickles leaves, a cheeky tease,
"Who's ripe today?" they giggle with ease.
Bumblebees buzz with tales to share,
While worms plot a dance in the cool night air.

Squirrels snicker, hoarding their stash,
While pumpkins blush at their Halloween bash.
Grapes argue who's sweeter on the vine,
"Come join us!" they cheer, "We're all divine!"

So in this harvest, don't take a nap,
Join in the fun, don't miss the clap!
For the secrets of sweet, juicy cheer
Are best shared among friends, gather near!

Echoes of Nature's Embrace

In the grove, voices collide,
Fruits gossip with pride worldwide.
Peaches claim they're the fluffiest pair,
While cherries argue they don't need a hair!

Rustling leaves hold a secret dance,
A plump fig winks, "Give life a chance!"
Berries caper with speckled glee,
"I'm the dessert!" shouts a proud kiwi.

The sun chortles with morning light,
"Harvest your humor, hold onto tight!"
Nature teases in shades of green,
Where laughter ripens, unseen but keen.

So if you're lost in the orchard's maze,
Follow the chuckles, they'll guide your ways.
For when fruits gather, their tales will rise,
A juicy joke in nature's skies!

The Subtle Art of Ripeness

In silence, fruit ripens, slow but clear,
A pear winks, "Taste me, I'm near!"
Every tick of time, it readjusts,
While apples plot to avoid the dust.

"Hey, pomegranate, you look quite bright!"
"Thanks!" it replies, "I'm ready for the bite!"
Bananas peel laughter from their skin,
"Join our party, let the fun begin!"

The art lies in the subtle shades,
Nature's palette where humor pervades.
Fruits laugh at the clocks, don't take a fall,
For the world's ripe jest is for one and all!

So if you nibble a sweet, tasty treat,
Remember the fun where flavors meet.
In the orchard's embrace, let your heart delight,
For ripes and jokes make everything right!

Tales from the Fruitful Arc

Gather 'round, listen close, my friends,
Fruits unite, where the laughter never ends.
Oranges giggle with zesty cheer,
"I'll zest your life, come over here!"

Lemons chime in, "We're sour but bright,
A squeeze of our joy makes everything right!"
Plums dance in purple, flouncing their skirts,
While berries tease about all their flirts.

Pineapples wear crowns, so bold and grand,
"Join our royal fest, lend us a hand!"
On watermelons, secrets swirl,
As honeydews make plans to twirl.

Every fruit has a tale to tell,
Of sunny days and soaked in sweet smell.
So come take a seat in this fruity bazaar,
Where laughter twinkles like a shooting star!

Soft Echoes of the Orchard

In the grove where fruits jest,
A little pear plays dress-up,
Sways in breezes, thinks it's best,
Chasing birds with a hiccup.

Trees gossip their leafy tales,
While the wind shares silly quirks,
Bouncing off their barky scales,
As the sunlit orchard smirks.

Caterpillars throw a dance,
While bees buzz tunes, oh so sweet,
Nature's little rom-com chance,
With leaves twirling on their feet.

Maybe next time, bring a friend,
To the orchard, wild and free,
With laughter's echoes that won't end,
In this land of jubilee.

Secrets Held in Sunlit Shadows

Underneath the dappled sun,
Secrets laugh beneath the tree,
A pear's prank has just begun,
Tickling limbs with glee and spree.

Squirrels giggle, and they tease,
Swapping acorns, mischief reigns,
When the breeze stirs up the leaves,
A chorus of squeals remains.

In shadows, whispers softly glide,
As the sun blushes and sways,
With every riddle, plants confide,
To the roots that dance all day.

Grab a seat, watch the show,
Where strawberries chuckle and roll,
In a world of fun, we'll go,
For nature hides a jolly soul.

Lingering Sonnet of the Grove

In the grove, the laughter flows,
Leaves erupt in fits of fun,
Meet a pear who sunbaths, glows,
Winks at all, it's joking run.

Bees take breaks at dinner time,
Sipping nectar with a grin,
While the fruit roams, out to mime,
This is where good times begin.

Birds are jesters, tails a-flair,
They serenade the afternoon,
Every critter stops to stare,
At the comical festoon.

So let's share a laugh or two,
In this fruitful, jolly plight,
With quirky fruits and stories new,
Chasing away the fading light.

Gentle Words of the Harvest Moon

Underneath the harvest glow,
Whispers fly in night's embrace,
Pears swing low, putting on a show,
With giggles woven in each case.

Moonlight beams on fruit so sweet,
Shining down on silly pranks,
Every bump's a dancing feat,
Through the grove, the laughter cranks.

Chubby rabbits paint the scene,
Bouncing cheeks and fluffy tails,
As canopies sway green to sheen,
In moonlit dreams, the humor sails.

Join the waltz with pies in tow,
As we crop the silly night,
In this world where giggles grow,
Beneath the moon's warm, silver light.

Soft Murmurs of Nature

In the orchard where the fruit hangs,
The bushes chuckle, the tree trunk clangs.
A babbling brook tries to join the chat,
While ants parade in a dandy hat.

Bumblebees buzz gossip on the breeze,
Whispers of snacks hidden under the leaves.
A squirrel juggles acorns with flair,
While butterflies dance without a care.

The grass stands tall, hoping for a joke,
A cactus grins, but he's just a hoax.
Nature's playhouse thrives on the silliness,
Where even the roots get caught in the stress.

The Language of Ripeness

In a world where fruits start to chat,
Bananas gossip, 'Is that a cat?'
Apples chuckle as they hang with glee,
'Who's stealing our shine? Let's wait and see!'

Citrus squabbles over the juiciest lines,
'The zest of life is in pair of limes!'
Berries tickle each other with puns,
Fruits in a frenzy, oh what fun runs!

A watermelon rolls over, oh what a sight,
'Check out my stripes, aren't they just right?'
They trade silly stories of sun and rain,
In this fruity realm, laughter never wanes.

Lessons in Sweetness

Life's a lesson taught by the sweet,
A peach shimmies, saying, 'Can't be beat!'
The honeydew rolls in, round and bold,
Telling tales of sweetness yet untold.

Strawberries wink and concoct a plan,
To knock the sour with a cheeky span.
Every fruit here plays a savvy game,
Making joy their only claim to fame.

Jokes aplenty in this juicy land,
With each burst of laughter, fruits take a stand.
Life is sweeter when we share the fun,
So join in the laughter, don't just sit, run!

Shadows of the Orchard

In the orchard where shadows stretch wide,
Grapes giggle softly, they take it in stride.
'What's that over there, oh what a fright!'
'Just an apple rolling, it's lost its sight!'

The trees play hide and seek in the sun,
While the mushrooms sit back, and just have fun.
'You call that a shadow? Check out my pose!'
Ripe laughter echoes from trunk to those toes.

Even the clouds can't help but chuckle,
As they prod the sunlight, making it buckle.
With every breeze, a secret is tossed,
In this shadowy realm, no humor is lost.

Golden Memories of Fall

In the orchard, laughter rings,
As fruits drop down with funny flings.
Leaves dance on the breezy air,
Jokes are shared without a care.

Squirrels chattering, quick in pace,
As they race around the place.
One slips, lands with a fruity thud,
And rolls away into a mud.

Golden hues paint every tree,
As pumpkins giggle, quite carefree.
The harvest moon shines on the fun,
As laughter spreads, it can't be done.

Memories fade but leave a stain,
Of joyful times, like a fruit rain.
Each bite a laugh, each crunch a cheer,
In the orchard, autumn's near.

Beneath the Fruitful Canopy

Underneath the branches wide,
Where silly creatures come to hide.
A raccoon dances, shakes his tail,
While birds compete to tell a tale.

With ripe sides leaning to the ground,
The fruits all whisper, secrets found.
They chuckle softly, what a sight,
As ants parade, with snacks in flight.

The wind plays pranks, it sways just right,
Fruits topple down, a comical sight.
They bounce and roll, a merry race,
As kids chase giggles, join the chase.

Beneath this leafy, fruitful dome,
Laughter fills the world like foam.
With every crunch, the giggles spread,
As fruit and fun go hand in hand.

The Dance of Lush Green

In a field where green does sway,
The flowers chuckle, bright and gay.
They twirl and spin, a silly sight,
While bees laugh hard, in pure delight.

Dandelions puff some air,
As they float 'round without a care.
The grass does tickle toes that roam,
Inviting all to call it home.

The sun winks down, a cheeky beam,
Turning life into a dream.
As shadows play and giggles chase,
All join in a merry race.

In this realm of green so bright,
Every moment brings pure light.
Where laughter flows like streams of gold,
And silly stories are retold.

Whispers of Nature's Bounty

In the garden where secrets bloom,
Nature's whispers fill the room.
A pumpkin waves, a squash with flair,
They share their jokes without a care.

Tomatoes chuckle, red and round,
As zucchini plays a hiding sound.
With cucumber comedies, they pair,
While carrots giggle, unaware.

But bees swarm in, just like a crew,
Comedians buzzing, that much is true.
They buzz about, with laughter sweet,
Flipping stories with every beat.

In this bounty, joy is found,
With fresh delights that spin around.
Nature's laughter fills the air,
Making moments beyond compare.

A Tapestry of Sweetness

In a garden where laughter grows,
Fruits wear smiles, as everyone knows.
Jokes on branches, ripe to see,
A fruity dance, come join with glee.

Juicy secrets tucked away,
Whispers of sweetness, come what may.
The trees chuckle, the soil grins,
Comedy's ripe, let the fun begin!

Beneath the sun, a playful breeze,
Winks at the pears, with utmost ease.
Their playful puns add zest to days,
In this fruity world, hilarity plays.

So grab a slice, let laughter swell,
In every bite, there's a story to tell.
A tapestry woven in nature's scheme,
With every giggle, we live the dream.

Savoring Silence

In orchards still, where silence sings,
The fruits plot mischief, with silly wings.
Giggling softly, they sway in mirth,
Beneath the stars, they find their worth.

A blushing blush on cheeks that shine,
Nature's humor in the vine.
They slide on dew, with beaming grace,
To dance in quiet, a giggly chase.

Crickets chime a whimsical tune,
As fruit confesses under the moon.
In hushed tones, they share their tales,
Of silly spills and fruity fails.

As dawn creeps in with waking light,
Laughter spills, oh what a sight!
In silent joy, they find their place,
In every heart, a fruity embrace.

Chasing the Dreams of Fall

As autumn comes with golden cheer,
The fruits plan mischief, have no fear.
With leaves like laughter, they caper and spin,
Chasing their dreams in a fruity grin.

They wear their colors, bold and bright,
In this merry dance of pure delight.
Crimson apples roll and laugh,
Whispering secrets, their fruity craft.

Pinecones chuckle, squirrels join in,
While pumpkins round, they easily win.
A race of glee through fields so tall,
In this whimsical chase, they'll never fall.

So let the laughter swirl and sway,
As fruits and nuts join in the play.
Chasing dreams 'neath the autumn sky,
With silly antics, we laugh and sigh.

Melodies of the Season's End

As winter whispers, fruits gather round,
In a chilly chat, their jokes abound.
Snowflakes giggle, and the branches sway,
As they share stories of their heyday.

A snowman dances, fruit hats on top,
Creating laughter that'll never stop.
Bananas slip and slide with glee,
In this joyous end, how sweet to be.

With frost nipping at their cheek,
They warm their hearts with words unique.
In the quiet, melodies blend,
Of frosty fun, here's a note to send.

As the season bows, with spirits high,
Let's raise our voices to the sky.
Together we laugh, we hum, we sing,
In this fruity world, joy's everlasting fling.

Soft Echoes of Nature's Lullaby

In the garden, a chatter that's nearly absurd,
A melon told a joke; the laughter was heard.
Tomatoes rolled over, their seeds in a spin,
While cucumbers giggled, their fun had begun.

The daisies all danced, with a sway and a shake,
As carrots turned red from the jokes they can take.
A fruit salad party, oh what a delight,
With laughter and chatter that lasted all night.

Tones of Sweet Harvests

A ripe apricot claims it's the star of the show,
While lemons just pout, 'cause they're sour and slow.
Berries are busy, they're causing a scene,
Wearing tiny hats, looking so very keen.

The corn likes to whistle, so loud and so clear,
While radishes blush, they can't handle a cheer.
Fruits in the basket all jostle for space,
Saying, 'Pick me, oh pick me!' with a cheeky grace.

Fragrant Memories of Autumn

As pumpkins wore scarves, quite fashionable too,
The apples all giggled, they knew just what to do.
Chill in the air but warmth in the heart,
While sweet little pearts play the comedy part.

The acorns don't laugh, they have troubles to pout,
But chestnuts roll over and help them out.
Squirrels, with acrobats, leap through the leaves,
While nature plays pranks, and everyone believes.

The Glistening of Hidden Fruits

Beneath leafy canopies, mischief unfolds,
Strawberries giggle, hiding gems like pure gold.
Kiwi hops merrily, full of delight,
While oranges play peek-a-boo, 'til it's night.

The laughter of fruits fills up every nook,
With cherries who whisper, "Come read us a book!"
All play in the shadows, with whispers and cheer,
Creating a tale that we love to hold dear.

Unspoken Promises in the Canopy

In the branches, secrets dance,
As fruit giggles in a trance.
Leaves chuckle in the breeze,
While squirrels plot their little threes.

An apple hangs with cheeky flair,
Winking at the pear with flair.
Laughter echoed, no one knows,
What mischief in the orchard grows!

A funny thought of nature's game,
Who's the silliest? Who's to blame?
The shadows play, the sunlight pranks,
In this orchard, we give thanks!

With every rustle, whispers sit,
Sweet fruits unite in witty skit.
Oh, the canopy, so lush and grand,
Holds the laughter of fruit and land!

Conversations of Shadows and Light

In the garden, shadows meet,
Sunflowers boast of feeling neat.
"Did you hear the squash's joke?"
Laughter ripples, light to poke.

The cucumber, quite a clever chap,
Tells a tale while taking a nap.
"Was I a salad or a side?"
Germinating giggles wide.

In every gleam, a story spins,
Where tomatoes grumble, rhyme begins.
"Pickle me this!" the radish shouts,
As root jokes flourish, no doubts!

A dance, a spin in sunlit shade,
Conversations in the glade.
With shadows whispering secrets tight,
Nature's comedy, pure delight!

Embrace of Autumn's Mellow Touch

Leaves tumble down in jolly hues,
While pumpkins sport their vibrant blues.
Squirrels stash acorns with flair,
Chasing gold in the crisp fresh air.

The harvest sings in giggly tones,
As wind plays tunes on weathered stones.
"Is it time for cider?" apples tease,
In frolics as they sway with ease.

Corn stalks rustle with a grin,
As autumn calls the kites to spin.
Chasing leaves, oh what a sight,
In this wacky, warm twilight!

With every burst of orange bright,
Nature's laugh brings pure delight.
So gather 'round, let's not rush,
In autumn's hug, there is a hush.

The Tongue of Fruitful Abundance

Fruits of all hues take to the stage,
Ripe and silly, they engage.
"Pick me, pick me!" berries proclaim,
In this wacky, juicy game.

Banana peels in playful slips,
Grapes giggle with juicy quips.
"Who can bounce the highest today?"
As fruity fellows laugh and play.

Every harvest sings a tune,
Underneath the harvest moon.
With each bite, a giggle shares,
Fruits unite in comedic flares.

So gather 'round, have some fun,
Let's toast to fruits, each everyone!
In this abundance, joy unfolds,
As laughter peaks, the story's told!

An Ode to Juicy Secrets

In the orchard where fruits reside,
A chatty fruit that cannot hide.
With a giggle and a gleam,
Saying, 'I'm sweeter than a dream!'

Laughing leaves dance in the breeze,
As quiet squirrels do as they please.
Spilling tales of ripe delight,
While bugs buzz 'neath the moonlight.

Juicy tales from boughs so bright,
Sneaking snacks in the dead of night.
Biting into tart debates,
About who holds the juiciest traits.

So the fruits, in playful jest,
Share their shades and who's the best.
A fruit feast that's full of cheer,
With juicy secrets whispered near.

Whispers Among the Ripening

As the sun warms the leafy chairs,
Fruits begin their gossip pairs.
'Have you seen the green ones pout?
They think we're sweet, but have no clout!'

Grapes giggle, hanging in bunches,
Cracking jokes, sharing hunches.
'Plum is so proud with her round face,
But she rolls when she's in a race!'

Beneath a sky so blue and bright,
Banter grows, a comical sight.
Juicy, ripe, they tease and brag,
While nearby, an apple drags.

In the orchard, mischief thrives,
As laughter fuels their sunny lives.
Each whispered word, a juicy jest,
Ripe with mirth, they jest their best.

The Sweetness of Silence

In the hush of the morning gleam,
A quiet squash had a wild dream.
'What if, just once, we made a sound?
A burp, a squeak, from underground!'

While fruits shy away from their fate,
The pears wink, daring them to state.
'They're all sweet, but I've got the trick,
To tickle your tongue and make it slick!'

In the stillness, sudden hiccups arise,
Giggling fruits in a funny disguise.
Cucumbers chuckle as they delight,
In a symphony of silent bites.

Oh, the sweetness of zipped-up thoughts,
Fruits pondering their playful blots.
A banquet of comical, ripe surprise,
They challenge silence with joyful cries.

Rituals of the Orchard's Breath

As dawn breaks in glittering light,
Fruits gather for a jesting fight.
With a wink, the cherries confer,
'Let's see who can cause a stir!'

A ritual dance beneath the breeze,
Where bananas spin with such ease.
'Who's the silliest in this crowd?
Lettuce laughs; he's always loud!'

Quirky rituals of ripe delight,
With every twist, they spark joy bright.
'Watch that pear—he's up to no good!
Plotting mischief in the wood!'

In this orchard, the laughter flows,
Each fruit's antics garnering shows.
With every giggle, the sunlight swells,
In a world where sweet chaos dwells.

Secrets of the Swaying Boughs

Up in the tree, a secret's spun,
The boughs are giggling, oh what fun!
A squirrel's dance, a leaf's quick dive,
They chuckle about how they'll survive.

Beneath the moon, they share their dreams,
Of fruit-filled days and berry creams.
The breeze plays tricks, a playful tease,
As laughter rustles through the leaves.

Each swing and sway, a jest to share,
With cheeky whispers hiding in the air.
The branches bounce with every jest,
In nature's chorus, they are blessed.

And when the wind gets just too bold,
They swap their tales of courage told.
From seeds of laughter, joy takes flight,
Under the stars, they laugh all night.

Subtle Hues of Autumn

Autumn leaves, in colors bright,
Giggle as they take their flight.
From red to gold, they dance and spin,
In this season's fun, they always win.

A pumpkin rolls, all round and plump,
It bumps along, a cheerful thump.
The scarecrow yawns, "What a silly day!"
The harvest moon has come to play.

As cider brews in jugs so wide,
The apples join, they laugh and bide.
With every sip, they spill a tale,
Of merry moments in the gale.

And all around, the buzz is heard,
With every gust, the laughter stirred.
In the subtle hues, they bask and joke,
Autumn's charm, a funny cloak.

A Harvest of Quiet Tales

In the orchard, whispers roam,
Giggling fruits claim this as home.
With every rustle in the breeze,
A tale emerges from the trees.

Cherries chime with a jolly tune,
While crickets chirp beneath the moon.
One pear insists it's quite the star,
But plums roll by, saying, "Not by far!"

As shadows stretch with the setting sun,
All gather 'round, it's story fun.
The pumpkins chuckle, "We're so fine!"
While zany squash form a straight line.

With every laugh, the night grows rich,
In those quiet tales, they find their niche.
So join the harvest, let the fun prevail,
For laughter's fruits never grow stale.

Whispering Leaves Beneath

Underneath the leafy crown,
The whispers start, but never drown.
Each fluttering sound, a hidden joke,
As laughter melds with the gentle cloak.

The acorns gossip, "Did you see?
That wobbly bark, it fell from a tree!"
While twigs creak with stories to tell,
Of mishaps with a windy swell.

Beneath the branches, fun abounds,
Especially where the laughter sounds.
The grass sways proud, takes part in jest,
Bartering chuckles like a quest.

With every rustle, tales take flight,
In the hush of leaves, they dance at night.
So come, embrace the merry truth,
In nature's giggle, we find our youth.

Secrets of the Blooming Bough

In the orchard, pranks unfold,
Each branch a tale, both bright and bold.
A squirrel plots with sneaky flair,
While apples giggle, hanging there.

Lemons tease the oranges near,
Chortling softly, spreading cheer.
A secret pact beneath the sun,
Where fruit and laughter blend as one.

In shadows, grapes start a dance,
With winks and swirls, they take a chance.
Peaches chuckle, giggle, and sway,
In a fruity, funny cabaret.

Ode to mischief grown on trees,
Nature's jest, a playful breeze.
When blossoms bloom, the fun takes flight,
In the boughs, everything feels right.

A Gentle Language of Fruit

Citrus speaks in zesty tones,
Where lemons tease the chatting cones.
Berries blush in a merry crowd,
Underneath a leafy shroud.

Bananas laugh from high above,
Swinging low, in a playful shove.
Peers gather close with cheerful cheer,
As laughter ripples through the sphere.

Cherries gossip, sweet and round,
In every glance, more fun is found.
A juicy code in vibrant hues,
Where nature shares its silly views.

With whispers soft, they share their dreams,
In fruity phrases and giggly beams.
Each word a sparkle, each joke a treat,
In this garden, every day's a feat.

Veiled Conversations at Dusk

When evening paints the sky with glee,
Fruit whispers secrets, soft and free.
The darkness holds a playful tune,
As cherries plot beneath the moon.

With shadows thick, the berries scheme,
In twilight's glow, they live the dream.
A mischievous fig rolls down the hill,
In fits of laughter, they're never still.

Apples gossip as they sway,
Trading jokes at the end of day.
The air is filled with chuckles bright,
In this dusky, playful delight.

With each soft breeze, they share a laugh,
A harvest of joy in nature's path.
In hidden nooks, they joyfully play,
Veiled conversations—nature's display.

The Silken Voice of Nature

In the morning light, the fruits awake,
Softly trading tales they make.
Breezes carry giggles high,
While pears and plums spark a sly reply.

With a rustle here and a sway right there,
Each fruit confesses with tender care.
A pun from the peach, a jest from the fig,
Their humor flows, both sweet and big.

Waves of laughter roll through the grove,
Where nature's voice will gently strove.
With every crunch, a story blooms,
Within the shade of leafy rooms.

From sunshine's glow to twilight's end,
Fruits weave a story, they never bend.
In the silence, their jokes take flight,
A silken voice that feels so right.

The Delicate Dance of Ripening

In orchards green, a waltz unfolds,
With fruits so round and tales untold.
They jiggle as the breezes blow,
Dancing softly, putting on a show.

The sun has set, a disco ball,
While squirrels groove, having a ball.
With every jig, the laughter grows,
A fruity party, everyone knows!

Peeling laughter, laughter so sweet,
Round and yellow, what a treat!
As they ripen, what a sight,
Pears prancing in the soft moonlight.

So grab a snack, enjoy the fun,
In this dance, we've just begun!
With every smile, and every sway,
Nature's party comes out to play!

Secrets Carved in Fruit

Whittle me a secret, oh fruit divine,
With every bite, a story's line.
Juicy whispers in every slice,
A crunchy giggle, oh so nice!

In the orchard's hush, a tale unwinds,
Of juicy laughter that nature finds.
Slicing through with zest and flair,
Each piece holds giggles beyond compare.

So gather round, let's share a laugh,
With every fruit, we split in half.
Delight in nature's giggly art,
In every bite, we play our part.

These fruity tales do make us beam,
In every crunch, a silly dream!
Savor secrets as we munch,
Laughter bubbles in every lunch!

The Lure of the Lush Path

Follow the path where laughter rolls,
With fruits so bright, they steal the souls.
A winding trail, with giggles loud,
Where every step lifts up the crowd.

Beneath the boughs, mischief sways,
As fruits pretend they know the ways.
Upon the ground, they find their glee,
Rolling 'round, as silly as can be!

The laughter echoes, sweet and clear,
As cheerful fruits draw us near.
A lush parade, with every bump,
Leading to a joyful jump!

So skip along, embrace the fun,
In nature's heart, joy's on the run.
Each twist and turn, a hearty laugh,
In this lush path, we craft our craft!

Voices of the Abundant Trees

The trees stand tall, they tell their tales,
With rustling leaves and giggly gales.
Roots that wiggle, branches that sway,
In this leafy realm, we play all day.

"Hey there, friend!" the branches tease,
"Come join our fun, it's sure to please!"
With fruity friends all gathering round,
What silly sounds can here be found?

A jolly chorus of nature's beat,
With every chirp, a joyful treat.
Abundant trees with laughter loud,
Invite us in, a friendly crowd!

So join the dance, let spirits fly,
With trees and fruits, we'll touch the sky.
Each voice a spark of pure delight,
In this merry wood, all feels right!

Fruits of Secrets

In the orchard where laughter bounces,
Fruits conspire with sly little flounces.
A cheeky apple, a grape with a grin,
Whispers sweet nonsense, let the fun begin!

Bananas chuckle, swaying with glee,
While oranges plot mischief on a spree.
"Peel us if you dare!" the lemons do tease,
As they roll from their branches, down to their knees!

Cherries giggle, hanging in a row,
Plotting the pranks they're ready to show.
With leaves for their hats, it's a grand masquerade,
Playing hide and seek in the sun's golden shade.

A fruity parade where secrets bloom bright,
In the quirky orchard, oh what a sight!
Laughter and juice mix in the air,
Fruits of delight, with mischief to share!

Echoes in the Orchard

In the orchard, chittering echoes arise,
Fruits whisper secrets under blue skies.
Watermelons rolling, like giggly old fools,
While peaches throw parties in leafy cool pools.

"Did you hear what that kiwi just said?"
"Not a clue," said the tomato, "I'm turning red!"
Bananas are dancing, giving all they can give,
While lemons demand all the credit they live!

Chubby cherries burst forth in their glee,
Squealing with laughter, they climb up a tree.
The figs play a tune, strumming their dreams,
As the apples roll by, plotting silly schemes.

Through branches and breezes, the giggles expand,
Echoes of humor flow hand in hand.
In this fruity carnival, joy is the king,
As each juicy heart has a sweet song to sing!

Soft Murmurs of Harvest

As the harvest moon grins wide and bright,
The fruits gather whispers in the soft night.
Mangoes gossip about their smooth skin,
While carrots chuckle thinking they'll win!

Cabbages giggle, draped in their greens,
Debating who's best with their muddy routines.
While berries boast of their sweet, juicy fame,
The pumpkin just smiles, glad it's never lame.

In corners unseen, laughter takes flight,
As nuts tell their tales by the pale moonlight.
"Join the fun!" croaks the frog in the patch,
As fruits roll about, making quite the catch.

With whispers and chuckles that dance through the air,
Soft murmurs of harvest, a fruity affair.
Each note of laughter resounds with delight,
In nature's confetti, everything feels right!

Beneath the Leafy Veil

Beneath the leafy veil, secrets are spun,
Fruits share their stories; oh, this is fun!
A cantaloupe caper with a slice of surprise,
And berries in hiding, sporting bright ties!

The grapes giggle softly in clusters so bold,
While apples claim fame with their tales often told.
"Oh dear!" whispers kiwi, "Don't roll in the dirt,
For if you do that, you might get hurt!"

Strolling through shadows, the fruits laugh and play,
With leafy companions who decide on the way.
"Let's throw a party!" the coconut shouts,
As passionfruit jigs, while the laughter flouts.

Under the branches, the fun is alive,
With quirky fruit legends that seem to thrive.
Beneath the leafy veil, they flutter and flail,
In the orchard of laughter, they happily sail!

The Song of Sweetness

In a garden full of cheer,
Fruits chatter, oh so near!
Bouncing jokes from tree to tree,
Laughing leaves, wild and free.

A yellow friend with a cheeky grin,
Sings of sun where laughs begin.
Tickling buds with playful tunes,
Underneath the smiling moons.

Squirrels dance with little flair,
While bees buzz tales of love in air.
A giggle ripples through the vines,
Nature's stage where joy aligns.

So take a bite of evening's snack,
Where humor, sweetness, never lack.
With every munch, a laugh to share,
In this bountiful, fruity affair.

Hidden Tales Among the Branches

Whispers float on breezy flight,
Branches hide tales from the light.
A secret joke from roots so deep,
Laughter's echo makes me leap.

A bough sways with a wink so sly,
"Why did the fruit refuse to fly?"
It tickled all the buds around,
As giggles danced upon the ground.

With every rustle, humor spreads,
As family of fruits share their threads.
Nutty jokes, a fruity spree,
In this green world, oh so free!

So raise your cup to branches wide,
For every laugh they do provide.
In hidden realms of nature's play,
Joy turns ordinary into a ballet.

Timid Threads of Nature's Speech

Among the leaves, a shiver shy,
Morning dew, a glimmering spy.
"Did you hear what the chill could say?"
"Just swiftly pass and join the fray!"

Fruits tremble at the breeze's jest,
While cheeky winds put them to test.
A timid giggle here and there,
As cherries muster up their flair.

A rustling voice calls on the air,
"Why wear a coat? It's not so rare!"
Snickering through the apple grove,
Nature's humor we all strove.

Listen close, the talk is sweet,
Tiny whispers, ripe and neat.
In timid threads, they stitch their fun,
Underneath the warming sun.

Cradled in Golden Light

In the soft embrace of sun's delight,
Fruits bask in a golden light.
"Do oranges laugh?" I ask in glee,
"Only when they roll, you see!"

Bananas swing and scold the breeze,
With jokes that bring the giggling trees.
"Lend me a laugh," the grapes all plea,
"Together we'll write nature's spree!"

A peach, so round, with humor sown,
Cracks a smile as seeds are thrown.
With every chuckle, joy takes flight,
In laughter's cradle, shining bright.

So in this garden, share a bite,
Where mirth and sweetness both ignite.
Cradled close in nature's hour,
Fruity jokes sprout like a flower.

www.ingramcontent.com/pod-product-compliance
Lightning Source LLC
Chambersburg PA
CBHW060140230426
43661CB00003B/502